IMAGES
of America
ROSLYN

"Miners from many countries answered the black diamond's call; / Men with a fearless courage sometimes with their backs to the wall. / In spite of cares and troubles and the hazardous lives they lived; / They were carefree, happy and always ready to give. / Scotch, English, Welsh, Irish, Slovaks, Italians and Poles; / They built the town of Roslyn and loved it heart and soul."

—Excerpt from *Wife of a Miner* by Anne Meyers Lennon

ON THE COVER: Miners gathered at the entrance to the old No. 5 mine in 1889. The miners wore open-flame coal oil lanterns on their hats. Before going down in the mine, miners filled up the base of their lanterns with coal oil and lit it. The open flame burned on top of their heads throughout the day as they worked. Open flames inside the mine were dangerous, given the accumulation of gasses underground. Miners, especially in the early days, worked in very dangerous conditions. Seated on the left end of the mine entrance is Robert Mayo, the great-uncle of Cmdr. Frances R. "Dick" Scobee (from Cle Elum), who after a celebrated career at NASA, was copilot of the space shuttle *Challenger* on January 28, 1986, when the O-rings failed on the solid rocket boosters and the shuttle and crew were lost. (Courtesy of the Roslyn Historical Museum Society, Inc.)

IMAGES
of America

ROSLYN

Jaymi Trimble

ARCADIA
PUBLISHING

Published by Arcadia Publishing
Charleston, South Carolina

Library of Congress Catalog Card Number: 2008928314

For all general information contact Arcadia Publishing at:
Telephone 843-853-2070
Fax 843-853-0044
E-mail sales@arcadiapublishing.com
For customer service and orders:
Toll-Free 1-888-313-2665

Visit us on the Internet at www.arcadiapublishing.com

*To Dad, Mom, Nana, Papa, Rick Adams ("Griz"),
Rusty Parton ("Mr. P"), and Leah—for always believing I would.*

*In memory of Dad, Nana, Jerie Trimble (my sister), Mr. P, and Arnie,
who watch over and encourage me from above.*

CONTENTS

ACKNOWLEDGMENTS

I would like to acknowledge the following:

God, through Him all things are possible.

Nick Henderson, president and curator of the Roslyn Museum, for all your hospitality and for opening your museum and archives up to me. Without you, this book would not have been possible. You have become my good friend, and I have loved every minute I spent at the museum. It is with heavy heart I finish this project, knowing the museum will no longer be my second home.

My mom, June Trimble, for moral support, encouragement, and countless hours babysitting while I completed this project. I love you, Mom!

My dad, James Wayne Trimble, who encouraged my love of history, supported me in following my dreams, and left me way too soon.

Nanna and Pappa, who always said having my nose in a book would some day pay off.

Lyndseigh Trimble Mahan, the best research assistant ever, for digging through thousands of old photographs, putting them away, and then doing it all over again after her technically challenged mother (me) scanned them at the wrong specs. Thank you for all the times you (willingly) played hooky during your senior year to help me on this project. And what a trouper, walking through thigh-deep snow several days in a row with me and Wolfie (freezing and soaking wet) to get information off of headstones. I love you very much!

Preston Trimble Mahan, my young marine, and Loegan Trimble Mahan for putting up with, and reluctantly giving over, their mommy to this project. Keep thinking Friesians, Loe! I love you both very much!

Leah Pate, my BFF, for 25 years of friendship—your smile, support (pushing and prodding!), and positive attitude have been there for me through many trying times. You are my NASA rocket scientist who lives NASA's "No Failure" motto in all areas of her life. I love you and Go Sooners!

Darren and Jilly Thompson, my dear friends, for loving and supporting me and for suggesting I visit Roslyn in the first place. I love you two very much.

C. Thomas Cooney, my Wolfie, who is such an amazingly talented photographer and iconographer. Thank you for all your trips to Roslyn—too many to count—and for helping me dig through the archives, picking and sorting through thousands of pictures. Also thanks for all the days we spent trudging through the deep, deep snow in the cemetery looking at headstone after headstone. It was through your knowledge of iconography that the headstones told the stories of the dead. I love you, Wolfie!

Jay DeBoer, thank you for countless hours of solving computer dilemmas, "Photoshop-ing" hundreds of images, and coming to Roslyn and taking photographs on numerous occasions.

My WSPIR family (Washington State Paranormal Investigations and Research, (www.wspir.com). You make me laugh and smile and so happy to be part of your lives. Thank you for all the support and encouragement during this project. I love y'all!

A special thanks to my editors Devon Weston and Sarah Higginbotham for helping me through the process. You two are awesome!

Unless otherwise noted, all images are courtesy of the Roslyn Historical Museum Society, Inc.

FOREWORD

I grew up playing on the same street in Roslyn as my mother and aunts and uncles. Our family is Croatian, but there were Slovaks and also Russians on that short two-block street. The center of the universe in my world was Ducktown. The neighborhood got its name because everyone had chickens, ducks, and geese running free.

Me, my cousins, and the neighbor kids would all take off in the morning for the tailing piles left over from the mines—we called them rock dumps. On those piles, made so many years before by the hardworking coal miners, we would look for fossils and spend the day comparing who had the best ones. Some days were spent on the big rock dumps pushing as much dirt as we could down the side of the mounds with our butts and making dams in the creek. A few hours later, we'd break them and watch the water go downstream in a big flood, taking out all the dams we had built.

Other days we would find ourselves up on the ridge playing all day, not worrying about being home until supper time. We made some of the best forts up there—I'm sure Davy Crockett and Daniel Boone would have been proud of us. We played Cowboys and Indians and army. We beat the Germans every time. Once in awhile, we would wander far enough that we'd find ourselves on the backside of the ridge in the West Fork of the Teanaway climbing and playing on the sandstone outcroppings along the stream. What a time we had.

We rode horses all summer long. Some days we'd be gone from sunup to sundown. It was on those days that we would catch a little of my Aunt Joanne's Okie (Oklahoma) temper. I don't know what she worried about . . . the horses always knew the way home.

Sometimes we'd play *Man from U.N.C.L.E.* in Pete's Wrecking Yard. It didn't matter if the bad guys shot us . . . we'd just put on some Speedy Salve (a fictional cure-all that fixed everything), and off we would go.

Once in a while, my brother and I would go over to Dale Morris's house and try imitating Beatles music. We had toy guitars and we'd use a pot lid to hang from something (like the vacuum cleaner) for the cymbals. There were only three of us, but we were so good we didn't need a fourth guy! Growing up in Roslyn in the late 1950s through the 1970s was a great place to be.

—Nick Henderson
President, Roslyn Museum Historical Society, Inc.

Nick Henderson (in rear) and his brother Rick ride their favorite horse, Patches. "Patches was one of those once in a lifetime horse," remembers Nick Henderson. "He was so gentle and patient with us kids. We rode that horse all over on our adventures. He'd always bring us home safe. There were plenty of times we lost track of time and space while playing and old Patches would get us back to the trail. He was a good old horse and I miss him."

Nick Henderson was born in Seattle and his family moved to Roslyn when he was an infant. He grew up in Roslyn and still resides there today. Nick is curator and president of the Roslyn Museum and also the cultural resource manager for Suncadia. He is active in the community, serving on numerous civic committees and boards.

INTRODUCTION

Roslyn, nestled in the Cascade Mountains, is a little town with a big history. The people of Roslyn, down through the generations, are what make the history of this pioneer town, founded three years before Washington was admitted to the Union, so remarkable. It was my pleasure to have the opportunity to tell Roslyn's story.

I intended to write a long introduction summing up the town's factual history. What I discovered while researching was much more interesting. Every day I spent at the Roslyn Museum was like being on a treasure hunt. I got lost in the history and discovered many amazing things. My glimpses back in time came from memoirs, newspaper clippings, city council minutes, and interviews. I learned about Roslyn's history from those who lived it.

During the past 122 years, Roslyn's residents have shaped and been shaped by the town's history, and although I found no photographs to go along with many of the stories, Roslyn's tale would not be complete without them. This book is limited in space, so I have narrowed our walk down Roslyn's memory lane to a few of my favorites. Join me in remembering: Roslyn's number one baseball fan, Artie Woods, who sat in the stands at every game and yelled, "Yip, Yip, Yip—Let's hit a home run—Yip, Yip, Yip" (Elaine Saxby also recalls Artie yelling words that she would get her mouth washed out with soap for repeating); the day the grand piano in the high school assembly room fell through the floor, leaving a gaping hole; the year Lake Cle Elum froze over and enough ice was cut by store owners to last the entire summer; Hub Cusworth's souped-up bobsled that would come racing down Catholic Hill, turn left at the Presbyterian church, and run all the way through town; sleigh rides to Lake Cle Elum covered with blankets—singing and laughing; the Halloween when one of the local stores' delivery wagons ended up on the high school roof; the year it snowed on the Fourth of July and all the kids ran their races in a heavy snowstorm; Friday night movies at the Rose Theatre and afterward a trip to the ice cream shop; swiping apples and lilacs on warm summer evenings while walking along the railroad tracks; when jelly beans and other candy really cost a penny at Mother Parollo's Candy Store on the corner across from the high school; all the things kids could find in the ditch that ran through town—a treasure trove of stuff they really needed, like wire wheels and old corset stays used to make bean shooters.

Other memories are recorded in city council minutes dating back to 1889. On July 12, 1889, city council voted to revoke F. T. Trottman's bond to operate a tavern because ladies of questionable character were entertaining in the back room of Trottman's saloon. On June 12, 1891, city council decided to pay damages in the amount of $100 to Oscar James after his house was knocked over by a fire hose while firemen were trying to put out a fire in the residence. On June 16, 1892, a certain secret society enclosed a large piece of land in the city cemetery and ran their fences within inches of other graves. Councilman Clark stated, "One dead person is as good as another even if they're not a member of a lodge." On November 17, 1892, it was agreed that someone would have to be hired to light the streetlamps at night because the night watchman was not reliable and had been spotted in various saloons drinking and playing cards while on duty, instead of keeping law and order and tending to the streetlamps. On April 8, 1895, Mayor William Adams reported he had received complaints that the marshal was allowing favored prisoners to go home at night to sleep. Mayor Adams stated he didn't think it was right for some to pay full penalty for their wrongs and others to be given special privileges. On June 24, 1895, the marshal was told to notify all persons having hogs, dogs, cattle, and chickens running loose through the city streets to pen them up or they would be put in the pound and owners would be charged to get them back.

I hope you will enjoy the photographs and stories in my book as much as I did. Roslyn is an amazing place, and I am honored to have had the opportunity to share her history with you.

—Jaymi Trimble
Roslyn, Washington, May 2008

One

WELCOME TO ROSLYN

After the discovery of immense coal deposits in the Cascades, the Northern Pacific Coal Company (a subsidiary of Northern Pacific Railroad) platted the town site of Roslyn in 1886. By 1895, Roslyn had everything from a justice of the peace and an attorney to a brewery, cigar factory, and a bawdy house. Roslyn was a rough mining town and one of the liveliest places in the state.

Coal mining began in Roslyn in 1886, when 550 miners were hired by the Northern Pacific Coal Company. Coal mining thrived, and immigrants came from all over the world to Roslyn to work the mines. They endured hard work and faced danger daily in the mines—injury and death were part of the job. Miners' wives worked hard at home doing household chores and raising the children. These men and women built the town of Roslyn.

During Roslyn's days of prosperity, the Northern Pacific Coal Company constructed the Roslyn Athletic Club for miners and their families. This became the town's main meeting place. The facility was completed in 1902 and contained a gym, dance hall, meeting rooms, and a bowling alley. Records from April 1910 show the club averaged 135 patrons per day, 110 people borrowed 350 books from the library, and 2,080 baths were taken at the club.

In December 1963, the Northern Pacific Railway permanently closed Mine No. 9, which was the last operating mine in Roslyn. This was the end of an era, as coal had been king in Roslyn since 1886. The economy suffered, and many people were left jobless. In a last-ditch effort to preserve Roslyn's coal-based economy, a local company made application for a government loan to keep the mine in operation. With no assured markets for the coal, the venture was deemed too risky and the application denied. Ironically, Roslyn is still sitting on over 230 million tons of coal.

In 1886, Logan M. Bullett, vice president of Northern Pacific Railroad, was given the task of naming the mining camp. When he moved west, he left his fiancée behind in Delaware. Logan missed her terribly and decided to name the town after her. There was great celebration over the naming—"Roslyn" was inscribed on a shingle and nailed to a pine tree at the edge of camp.

The New York Millinery sold items such as shirts, clothing, caps, aprons, hats, dresses, fabric, buttons, and lace. Women also took dresses to the milliner to be made over into something new. This photograph was taken in 1892. On the buggy are Ruth Merriman Fletcher and Clyde Merriman. Standing are Ruth Merriman Stoffer and Grandma Denny.

It's bottoms up for William Browitt in 1899 at the Brick Tavern. The Brick retains the feel of days gone by. During Prohibition, it was run as a soda fountain. However, if you played your cards right, you could get something more potent, as moonshine was smuggled in with coal deliveries. The 23-foot running water spittoon along the front of the bar is the only one still operating in the state.

Coal oil streetlamps were lit each night by a lamplighter. The lamplighter would come up the street carrying a ladder and a little can of coal oil. Stopping at each lamppost, he would adjust his ladder, climb up, and light the lamp. In the morning, he would return, put out the lamp, and clean it. He was paid $1 for each night he made his rounds. (Courtesy of Jay DeBoer.)

Bill Reese is remembered as a cantankerous Welshman who often sat working at his cluttered rolltop desk surrounded by rolls of linoleum, tar paper, and kegs of nails. He had a display of pocketknives that he kept padlocked. Most of the knives were bone handled and had two blades. A few had agate handles and four blades. Fifty cents could buy a bone-handled, two-bladed knife.

One of the earliest pioneers in Roslyn was a prospector named Nez Jensen. He built this cabin in 1885, and it is the oldest structure in Roslyn. When the town was platted, it was determined the cabin was on Northern Pacific land. The cabin was sold and used as a private residence until the 1990s, when the City of Roslyn bought the cabin and renovated it as a historic site.

The Rose Theatre was located on the lower floor of the Knights of Pythias Hall and showed double features every weekend. Grade schoolers paid 10¢, and high schoolers paid 15¢. Richard Hayes remembers, "One of my fondest memories as a kid during the summers in 1930 was the weekend movies which cost 10 cents at the Rose Theatre. The audience would exit at night and fade into the darkness. I'd wander over to The Brick, then down First Street and the carbon-arc street lamps would be flickering. If windy, they'd sway a bit. Very eerie. When I got back to my aunt and uncle's house, I'd let myself in with the hidden key and the regulator clock on the wall would tick-tock, tick-tock loudly. The silence of Roslyn and the hills was so deep that even as a kid you could hear the earth creaking as it turned on its axis." The building was destroyed by fire in 1943.

The Roslyn Bakery and Grocery opened in 1908 and was owned by Caesar Panieri. Caesar's grandson Jim Crestanello remembers, "Wood fires heated the bakery's ovens and bread baking time was between 1 and 2 a.m. The smell of baking bread filled the air. Around 2:30 a.m., in the pitch dark, my grandpa would load his wagon with bread and off he'd go to Ronald. Every night after delivering the bread, grandpa would climb back up in the wagon, go to sleep and the horse would take him home." During Prohibition, the Roslyn Bakery and Grocery sold a railcar load of sugar each month. This got the attention of federal agents from Seattle. Lemons and oranges, also used to manufacture bootleg whiskey, were being sold by the crate load. When the feds asked about this, Panieri told them his customers liked lots of sugar and lemon in their iced tea.

In November 1890, Roslyn had a new firehouse. In December 1890, city council voted to purchase a horse-drawn fire cart, 2 axes, 4 lanterns, 1 tool box, and 10 wrenches. It was six months later before the city could afford a fire hose, so until then, the Roslyn Volunteer Fire Department (above) continued to fight fires by bucket brigade.

The company store was the heart of the town for miners and their families. There they could purchase anything they needed—from groceries to clothes to lumber. What couldn't be had at the company store was ordered from the Sear's catalog. If there was work, a lantern would burn in the window of the store. Miners didn't have a set work week. Some weeks were better than others.

Coal mining towns, like Roslyn, were rowdy places where just about any vice could be found. In 1902, B. F. Bush, president of the Northern Pacific Railroad, built a place for miners and their children away from the taverns and brothels. The club, which eventually became the YMCA, included a bowling alley, swimming pool, gym, and a library. The club soon opened to all town residents.

John Bardesono (far left) purchased the German Bakery in the spring of 1901. Bardesono's specialty was torchetti—a horseshoe-shaped cookie made of puff pastry, glazed, flaky, and very tender. They were so popular it was impossible to keep up with demand and customers had to reserve them in advance. The ovens at the German Bakery were often used after hours to roast piglets, turkeys, lambs, goats, and geese for patrons.

In the late 1800s, when the Episcopal church was moved to its present location on a hilltop overlooking Roslyn, it was christened Calvary Church. There were a good number of priests who called Calvary home over the years. In the early days, mining towns were rough. Priests coming to Roslyn were warned that Roslyn was the worst. Roslyn's priests were kept plenty busy.

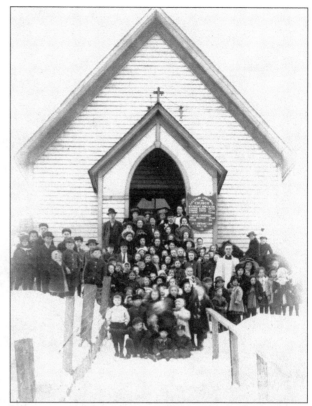

Steve Kuchin (in front) moved to Roslyn in 1900 from Austria and worked the mines until the 1909 mine explosion that killed 10 of his fellow miners. He felt he beat death because his crew was scheduled to work the shift after the explosion. Kuchin gave up mining and went into the grocery business. A 1914 advertisement described Pioneer Grocery as "The House of Value in Staples and Fancy Groceries."

In August 1890, the school board voted to borrow $5,000 to buy land and build a new schoolhouse. A portion of the money also had to be set aside to furnish the new school. Charles Adams was awarded the contract for a bid of $3,673.35. On April 2, 1891, school convened in the new schoolhouse for a term of three months, and there were 285 students between the ages of 5 and 21. It was noted in a ledger that the average cost per pupil per month was $12.12. Factored into this figure were teacher salaries, coal for heat, furnishings, and supplies.

Mrs. Maxwell helped Mr. McPherson decide what to purchase. Maxwell's Ice Cream Parlor had lots of goodies to choose from. There were glass cases filled with all kinds of goodies—ice cream, pie, chocolates, cake, candy, floats, and so on. A trip to Maxwell's was a real treat. There were also variety store gifts to purchase.

As reported in the *Cascade Miner* on October 23, 1897, "The miners are working six days a week, with some night shifts; improvements of all kinds are happening in the mines and everything goes to show that the white-winged dove of prosperity is preparing to again alight in the beautiful city of Roslyn." Coal was king in Roslyn for 80 years. There were good times thanks to the prosperity coal brought to the town, but also tragedy.

Before the first post office was established in Roslyn in 1887, mail was brought from Ellensburg on horseback when a rider happened to be heading that way. Thomas W. Fleming was Roslyn's first postmaster, and under his care, mail delivery became more regular and reliable. Pictured in 1916 are, from left to right, James Lane (postmaster), Julia Bugress, and Maud Allen.

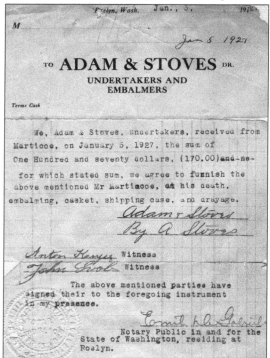

In 1892, Anthony Stoves Sr. opened a drugstore in a building he had recently built. Being an industrious businessman, he rented the second floor out as a lodge hall to Roslyn's numerous fraternal organizations. Behind the drugstore, he opened a mortuary and became Roslyn's newest undertaker.

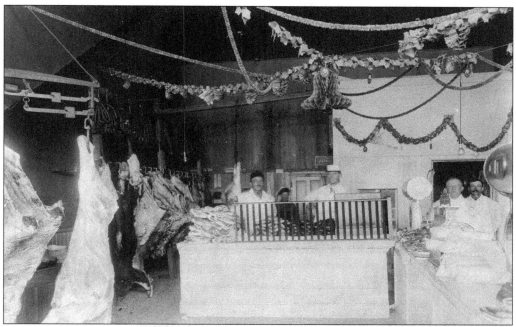

Welsh meat cutter Morgan Owen opened the Owen Meat Market in 1887. In 1987, the family received a letter from George Picatti of Yakima, "This is a long overdue letter of thanks. In 1904, I was three months old and Morgan Owen hired my 14 year-old brother after our father was killed in a tragic accident. Please accept our heartfelt appreciation for helping a widow woman and her three dependent children."

Mr. Hawthorne was killed in the 1909 mine explosion. Mrs. Hawthorne, suddenly a widow, had to support her children and decided to take in boarders. This was not uncommon for widows with children to feed. Widows were given a small compensation from the mining company—which wasn't even enough to even pay for funeral expenses. The Hawthorne House is currently a bed-and-breakfast called the Huckleberry House.

The Immaculate Conception Catholic Church was built in 1886. After the fire of 1888, the church was one of the few buildings that remained. For over 125 years, the church has been home to many different ethnicities that worship, marry, and have funeral services under the same roof. In the 1970s, the church was used by Stanley Kramer in his movie *The Runner Stumbles*, starring Dick Van Dyke.

Halstad Hotel was a boardinghouse for miners in the early 1900s. Amelia and Henry Labahn were the proprietors. Amelia is pictured on the left and Henry in the middle with his dog. Henry's sister Clara is pictured on the right. Clara died of the flu epidemic in 1918. Miners rented rooms by the week. Rent included room, two meals a day, and a bucket lunch. The hotel later burned down.

Two

LITTLE TOWN
WITH A BIG HISTORY

Roslyn's past is a tapestry of tales woven together over the past 122 years, which account for the town's remarkable history. Roslyn's historical heritage is rich, unique, and colorful. Some of the stories of Roslyn's past will amaze, others will shock. Here are two such stories:

Although there was a volunteer fire department in Roslyn, they had no equipment. On Sunday, June 22, 1888, about 4:00 p.m., a fire broke out in the Knights of Labor Union Hall and three blocks of town went up in a blaze. The only means of putting out the fire was bucket brigade. Billy Kitchen, who years later died when a huge piece of coal fell on him, recalled, "I helped form a bucket brigade that day. The water to put out the fire came from springs running along the streets. But after we bailed them dry, we just had to let the fire go." Many homes were burned and those residents lost everything—including one couple who had been married that day and all the bride had left was the wedding dress she was wearing. Those who were burned out moved in with those who had been spared. Within a short time, homes and businesses were rebuilt. Many of those buildings are still in use today.

During the strike of 1888, when mining companies brought in blacks to fill striking white miners' jobs, mob rule reigned. One Saturday, a black mining crew was working in a mine in Ronald when several "liquored up" whites went into the mine and randomly shot and killed several of the black miners. The mining company called the incident a "mining accident," although there was speculation as to what really happened from the beginning. No investigation was ever made, and the murdered black miners were immediately buried in a small cemetery in Ronald near the mine. And that was the end of it until 60 years later, when one of the men involved in the murders came forward and confessed the truth to clear his conscience.

Miners and loggers worked long hours and days off for these men were few and far between. In 1908, on a rare day off, Jimmie Hendry, Bill Moore, Bill Kinghorn, Bill Lumsden and Dan Lennon (from left to right) got together and went for a horseback ride.

Ever wonder how many bricks it takes to build a tavern? The Brick Tavern, built in 1889 by Fred Ruppert, took its name from the 45,000 bricks used to build it. The Brick (oldest operating tavern in Washington) offered miners booze, card games, pool, and bowling. The ornately carved bar was shipped from England, around Cape Horn of South America to Portland, then brought to Roslyn on a horse-drawn wagon.

During the summer, volunteer firemen rolled fire equipment to fires on carts. One hose cart was kept stationed on Catholic Hill. Once, during a fire, two firefighters raced up the hill to get the cart. On the way down, they lost control of the heavy cart, and it took off with them. They rolled by the fire so fast their coattails were flying in the wind behind them.

On a wall in the Roslyn Museum hangs a quilt made by fourth-grade students. The children cut, sewed, and embroidered their names on the quilt under the guidance of their teacher, Miss Farrell, in 1914. The quilt has 35 squares—one for each child in the class. (Courtesy of Jay DeBoer.)

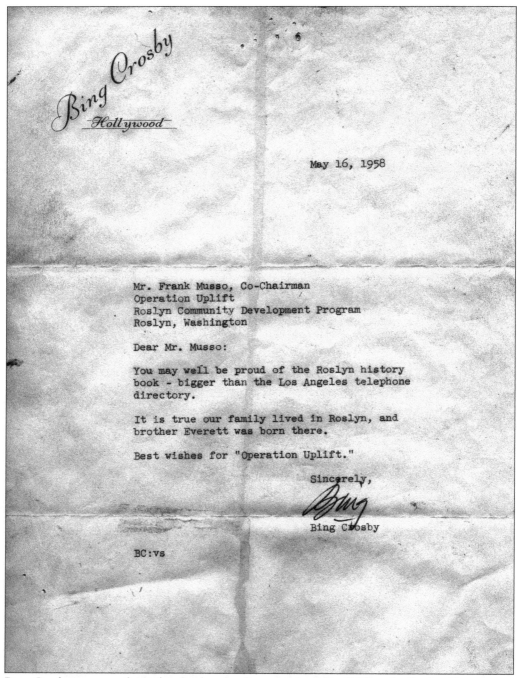

Bing Crosby
Hollywood

May 16, 1958

Mr. Frank Musso, Co-Chairman
Operation Uplift
Roslyn Community Development Program
Roslyn, Washington

Dear Mr. Musso:

You may well be proud of the Roslyn history
book - bigger than the Los Angeles telephone
directory.

It is true our family lived in Roslyn, and
brother Everett was born there.

Best wishes for "Operation Uplift."

Sincerely,

Bing Crosby

BC:vs

Bing Crosby never performed in Roslyn, but he sent a letter in 1958 to the Roslyn Community Development Program confirming that the family had lived there for a time and that Bing's brother Everett was born in Roslyn.

Former Roslyn mayor Neil McGovern remembered when the Yakima Indians came to Roslyn in caravans: "Lines of Indians could be seen a quarter mile long riding their horses and carrying spears. They'd set up their teepees along the Cle Elum River and play music and dance around the fire. Their days were spent fishing and picking berries to bring to Roslyn to sell." (Courtesy of Central Washington University.)

In Roslyn's early days, the biggest nuisances in town were the dogs, hogs, and cows running loose through the streets and cemetery. In 1895, the mayor ordered a pound built behind the jail. Stray dogs and livestock were rounded up and locked up by Kid Strong. For $1, they were released to owners, but the city was losing money because owners came under darkness and dug their animals out.

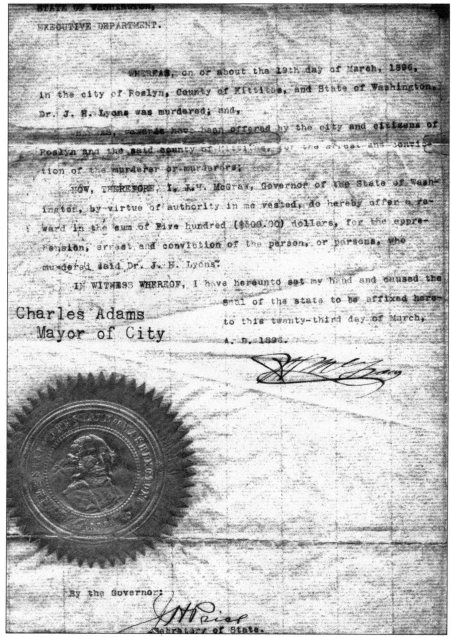

On March 19, 1896, Dr. J. H. Lyons was brutally murdered a few feet from his doorstep. Dr. Lyons was one of the earliest residents of Roslyn and had been the mining company doctor for many years. Dr. Lyons was well-liked, and his murder shocked the town. He was bludgeoned to death with a table leg that was found near the scene of the crime covered with blood and hair. Robbery was not the motive for the crime as Dr. Lyons's pocketbook, watch, and jewelry were found on him. A $500 reward was offered by J. W. McGraw, governor of the State of Washington, for the apprehension of Dr. Lyons's murderer; however, the mystery of who killed him remains unsolved. The notice of reward (above), dated March 23, 1896, still hangs in the Roslyn Museum.

In February 1916, Roslyn was snowbound in what is remembered as the "Year of the Big Snow." There was no way in or out of the town after 66.5 inches of snow fell in a 24-hour period. That brought the total snowfall that year to 385.5 inches. Many buildings were on the verge of collapsing from the heavy snow. The mines closed down for weeks.

In 1889, a coal miner, much in his cups, saw a rat scurry across his floor. He grabbed his shotgun, fired, and accidentally shot a powder keg he had in the house to keep it from freezing. He blew himself, his house, and the rat to kingdom come. The town fathers called an emergency meeting and passed a law banning the storage of powder kegs inside homes. (Courtesy of Jay DeBoer.)

Pictured are Jim Hawthorne (back row, center) and Matt Hawthorne (kneeling), who served their country during World War II. After leaving the military, Matt Hawthorne became an educator in Ronald; the school gym is named for him. In later years, he moved to Seattle, where he became a successful broker for Equitable Savings.

Young boys made a career of playing army and taking on the dreaded Germans during World War II. The boys, many who had brothers, fathers, or uncles overseas, did their part to protect freedom on the home front. Children of that generation were also very familiar with war rations and saw their mothers using ration coupons to support the war effort.

On May 18, 1929, Dr. Edward Heston, chief surgeon of the Roslyn–Cle Elum Beneficial Hospital, was on a fishing trip with friends when he accidentally slipped in the swift water of French Cabin Creek and drowned. He was remembered by Mayor Neil McGovern as "A good friend to all in the community—he did much for all of us. Many a night I was called out by Dr. Heston to assist him. I'd give the ether and he'd repair the fingers, operate for appendicitis, or deliver babies. On the night my son was born Dr. Heston said, 'Neil, we've been through this many times before. Let's go.' I gave Kate the ether and Dr. Heston delivered our ten pound boy. Then, Dr. Heston said, 'That deserves a drink,' and we got a gallon of wine and had ourselves a toot!"

TAKE THIS TO
THE ROSLYN PHARMACY
PRESCRIPTION SPECIALISTS
A. STOVES, Proprietor   ROSLYN, WASHINGTON

R For _m._   Address _Roslyn,_

Ung. analgesic   ℨ ii

M. Sig. Rub on.

27805

37804

E. S. Heston M. D.

40 P

FULL NAME

Address

Reg. No.   Date 2 8-1 4   Pres. No.

Roslyn had no idea that on September 23, 1892, it would go down in Old West bank robbery history ... but it did! Local legend has it that the masterminds of the robbery were none other than Butch Cassidy and the Sundance Kid. "It was him even though they never caught him!" exclaimed Frank Musso, founder and longtime curator of the Roslyn Museum. "A $40,000 payroll was arriving that day. Five armed men wearing bandanas rode up to the Roslyn Bank. The robbers didn't get the payroll, but made off with several thousand dollars—but not before pistol whipping several bank employees and shooting two people who tried to interfere with the robbery." Unknown to the bank robbers, the payroll had been taken from the train station to the mine office. After the robbery, many people decided to bury their money. For years, it was said there was more money buried in the ground than there was in the bank in Roslyn. (Courtesy of Jay DeBoer.)

Frank Musso (1894–1986), founder and former curator of the Roslyn Museum, was a lifelong resident of Roslyn. Musso had a tremendous passion for preserving Roslyn's history. As a kid, he worked at the Brick setting bowling pins by hand: "I started working at the saloon when I was 14. I'd work from 7:30 in the morning until midnight." Musso ran the museum from 1970 until his passing in 1986.

There was one passenger train a day that came through Roslyn. One morning in January 1919, a passenger railcar jumped the tracks just outside Roslyn. Passengers were jostled about, but no one was seriously injured. The worst part of the ordeal was waiting in the snow several hours while Northern Pacific moved in a crane to right the railcar. Once that was done, passengers re-boarded and were on their way.

This tree house, located on Seventh Street, was a popular hangout for boys. It was the one members-only club in Roslyn. The boys would spend all day plotting against make-believe foes—making dirt bombs and dragging buckets of pine cones up to fortify the fort so when the enemy attacked they would be ready. The branches on the tree next to the tree house served as the boys' ladder.

In the early 1900s, window shopping at Christmastime was popular with the children of Roslyn. Shopkeepers went all out with their window displays. Owens Meat Market had turkeys hanging from every hook. Maxwell's Candy Store was overflowing with holiday treats. The smell of fruitcakes filled the air from the German Bakery. For the boys, a window shopping trip was not complete without a gander at Reese's pocketknife display in the hardware store.

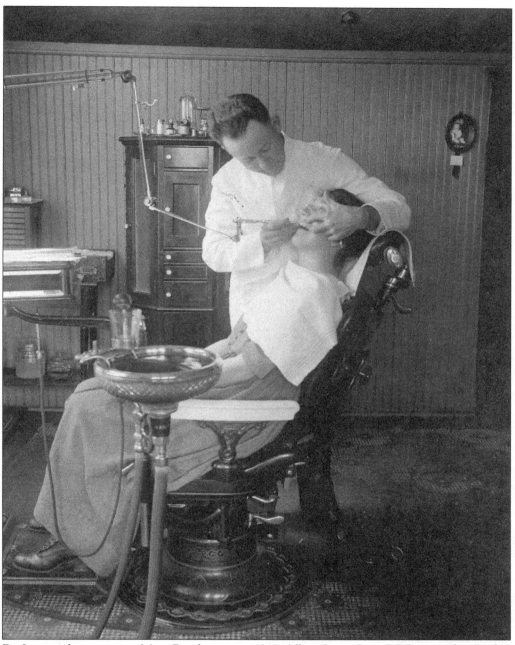

Dr. Low works on patient Mary Bovilacquia in 1910. Albert James Low, DDS, arrived in Roslyn on April 4, 1904. He described the place as a typical frontier town, except it had 24 saloons for the 24 different nationalities in town. He recalled that the tavern folk got wild after sunset on a regular basis, so there was never lack of excitement. Dr. Low remembered the music that would float through his window on Saturday nights from the various saloons: "Each of the saloons was frequented by immigrants from different parts of the world. I could sing the national anthems from many different countries because as the night wore on saloon patrons got drunk and sentimental and they'd stumble out of the bars singing their countries national anthems in the street."

Adolph Schlothfeldt was the owner of the Roslyn Brewery, and his niece Mayme Schlothfeldt remembered that as a child she would ride with her uncle on the brewery wagon. At each saloon, Adolph rolled in the barrels while Mayme, who was given two nickels at each stop, played the nickelodeon. The Roslyn Brewery closed during Prohibition but later opened under new ownership. (Courtesy of Roslyn Brewery.)

Ken Miller remembers that, as a boy, Frog Pond was the center of his world: "Someone has probably given Frog Pond a fancy name by now and cleaned up all the algae. The doctors didn't warn us back then about some dreadful disease that would result from coming in contact with the green stuff floating in the pond. Our whole summers were spent swimming in that pond. Those were the days."

During the winter months, groceries were delivered by sleigh from local Roslyn markets. The sleigh and team in the middle of the photograph belonged to John Bardesono of the German Bakery. Every day, driver and team would head out to make deliveries. Sometimes if a customer wasn't home, the driver would go in the house and put the eggs and milk away in the icebox. If the driver took too long, this team of horses, described by John Bardesono as "very frisky," would get tired of waiting and take off for the barn, leaving the driver to walk back to the store. This was particularly irksome in the winter when it was common for temperatures to be below freezing with 4 to 5 feet of snow on the ground.

Mary Andler was a fascinating source of Roslyn history. In 1960, she and her husband, Joe, donated the land for the Roslyn Museum. For 16 years, Mary was curator of the Roslyn Museum. She never forgot a detail and dedicated her life to preserving Roslyn's history. Mary passed away on Christmas Eve 2002, leaving a legacy of Roslyn history for generations to come.

Roslyn's mayor William Adams was also the town's undertaker. When his son William Adams Jr., a volunteer fireman, died in a 1909 hunting accident, he built a rack for the fire hose cart so the firemen could carry the body of his son to the cemetery. For many years afterward, all Roslyn's fallen firemen were taken to their final resting place on the hose cart.

Roslyn had a red-light district. It was located above what is today Lefty's and Ace Rental. The girls who lived there were known as "Girls of the Coal Mines." They were not allowed to walk on the streets, and on their days off, they had to leave town. In city council minutes from 1905, the town marshal was instructed to "confine the sporting women to the alley." They are remembered by several old-timers (who asked not to be named) as the "best dressed women in town." If readers look closely, they can see several of these "sporting women" standing on the balcony watching the 1901 Fourth of July parade. The balcony collapsed in the 1916 snow, and all that is left are the doors opening to nowhere.

Clustered on 15 acres of hilly pine forest are 24 separate, but adjacent, cemeteries that tell the story of generations past. In 1887, the Northern Pacific Company donated land for the cemetery, where people from 24 nationalities lie in their final resting place. By 1890, each nationality had its own fraternal organization to meet burial needs because miners received no benefits. The different nationalities were close in life and wanted to remain close in death. Burial customs from each country are represented with ornate tombstones, some with photographs of the deceased embedded in the marble, others surrounded by wrought-iron fences. There are countless graves of immigrants in the Roslyn Cemetery; each a reminder of the immigrants' contribution to the greatness of this nation. (Both courtesy of C. Thomas Cooney.)

Three

COAL IS KING

Coal, the "Black Diamond," was king in Roslyn for 80 years. To the residents of Roslyn, coal was life itself. Joe Venera remembers, "On my first day in the mines I survived a cave in. I'd load three cars a day for 80 cents a ton, come home covered from head to toe in coal dust and cough black stuff out of my lungs for hours . . . but I was lucky to have a job."

Miners made their living thousands of feet below the streets of the town, hacking out over a million tons of coal per year in Roslyn. It was brutal work, and there wasn't much reform in working conditions until the 1940s.

Mining was dangerous business. "Every time the wives and mothers of the miners would hear a siren, they'd run, breathlessly, from their homes to the ambulance and ask in fear if it was their husband or son inside who had been hauled from the mine," stated Frank Musso, former curator of the Roslyn Museum. Coal mining inspectors of the time reported loss of life and limb from calamities such as roof cave-ins, electrocution, falls, and numerous other causes brought on by poor working conditions. The potential for accidents was high. Inadequate mine ventilation was also a serious matter that took many a miner's life.

Ethel Craven remembered, "Every week it seemed someone would get killed or injured in the mines. The mournful whistle would blow and up the street would come the little ambulance wagon. And everyone wondered who it was that had been hurt or killed."

Despite the danger, miners returned to the mines day after day, year after year—so accustomed to danger that it became a way of life for them.

Roslyn was the site of the largest coal mining catastrophe in Washington State. At 2:00 p.m. on May 10, 1892, two boys were coming from inside the No. 1 mine with a donkey and a coal cart when a tremendous explosion occurred. The boys and the donkey were blown from the mouth of the mine. The boys survived a blast that killed 45 miners deep inside the mine. Around 5:00 p.m., hope turned to despair when the first bodies were brought out in a driving rain. Wives, children, mothers, fathers, brothers, and sisters stood in the mud and rain, crying. A morgue was set up at the fire station (above). It took rescue teams three days to recover all the dead. Several families lost fathers, brothers, and sons all in one day. The Cox children (left) were among the 91 children orphaned that day.

The funerals for the 45 miners were held on May 12, 1892. All businesses shuttered their windows out of respect for the dead, and the townsfolk lined Pennsylvania Avenue dressed in black to pay their last respects as the mass funeral procession passed. On the right side of this picture is the old fire hall with Roslyn's volunteer firemen standing at the ready to join the processional. A long line of 45 horse-drawn wagons carried the miners to their final resting place.

Despite diverse backgrounds, the immigrants—regardless of where they came from—were drawn together by the experience of working in the mines under dangerous conditions. Miners had to be able to count on their partners, regardless of color or nationality. Ethel Craven spoke of how blacks and whites worked together in the mines: "Men folk made comrades in the mines because when anything happened they would help one another, don't care what color you was." In the mines, everyone was equal. All miners and their families shared the same concerns regarding quality of life, work conditions, and the future of the industry by which they supported their families. (Courtesy of Jay DeBoer.)

This mule, named Gallagher, would only work six hours each day, but the miners had to work 10. When Gallagher's six hours were up, he refused to move. One day, the miners tied firecrackers to his tail to make him go. When the firecrackers went off, Gallagher took off like a shot. The miners said his tail looked like a pinwheel in the darkness of the mine.

In the late 1800s, it was common to see children going to the saloons to get buckets of beer for miners. Miners carried their lunch to work in buckets, and at the end of the day, they would turn their buckets over and fill them with beer. Beer cost a nickel a bucket. Miners got more beer by greasing their buckets so the beer wouldn't foam. (Courtesy of Central Washington University.)

The main shaft of the No. 9 mine goes down 2,700 feet. Once over the hump, the cars headed down the steep grade into the dark abyss at speeds up to 35 miles per hour. "Lots of times the engineer would forget to pull the clutch and we'd go down the shaft free-wheeling. It made your hair stand on end," remembers retired rope rider John Ferro. The mines were like cities underground—except they were dark. The tunnels went on for miles. The No. 9 mine had 54 miles of tunnels. The main tunnel was like Main Street, and the cross-cuts were like intersections. There were no lights in the mines because, as the coal cars were rolling along the tracks, coal would fly off and bust the lamps. John Ferro remembers the dark: "It was lighted a few hundred feet down and after that it was dark. I mean dark! The only light was that on your head and a light battery lasted for about 12 hours." (Courtesy of John Ferro.)

Rope riders rode between coal cars and had one of the most dangerous jobs in the mine. Everything that went into or out of the mine was the rope riders' responsibility. The rope rider belled the engineer, telling him where he wanted to go by reaching up and grabbing the electric lines with a rapper and tapping out a message while racing along at speeds up to 35 miles per hour—all while sitting on the edge of a railcar. "There was a signal for everywhere you wanted to go and everything you wanted to do," recalled John Ferro. "That's the only way the engineer thousands of feet above you knew where you and all the other rope riders were down in the mine. When signaling the engineer, you had to be fast or you'd be dead." (Courtesy of John Ferro.)

On Saturday, April 22, 1893, the *Roslyn News* reported, "The Northern Pacific Coal Company mined a 22 ton piece of coal—the largest ever cut—and sent it by rail to the Chicago World's Fair. The greater part of last week was spent working the immense block from the mouth of the mine and loading it on a railcar. It tipped the scale at 50,000 pounds."

After Roslyn's bank robbery, many people decided it was safer to bury their money. On his deathbed, a miner named Bettine tried to tell his wife where he had buried their money but died before he could get the words out. Years later, his sons decided to find the money. They dug until they found an old can full of money buried under the house. This house still stands on Fourth Street.

This is an excerpt from the 1912 Miner's Handbook: "Don't place too high a value on that last car of coal. Your life and limbs, as well as those who work with you, are of more value than all the coal you can mine in a lifetime. Also, don't neglect to prepare yourself that you may help to care for the injured in that accident which is almost certain to come at some time."

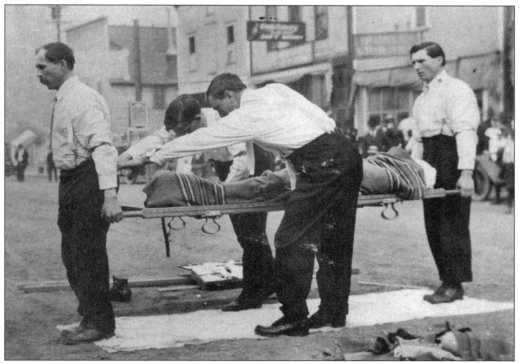

The Roslyn Mine Rescue Team stayed sharp by giving demonstrations for the public, as mine accidents occurred frequently. When an accident happened, a foreman would radio ahead on the downed miner's condition. John Ferro remembers, "When a miner got hurt everything came to a halt and focus was on getting the miner out."

Ten miners lost their lives on Sunday, October 9, 1909, when the No. 4 mine suffered a terrible explosion. Disaster is never far from the minds of those who have loved ones working in the mines. After the explosion, the streets were overrun with thousands of residents who didn't know who was lost. People ran screaming and praying toward the shaft. The city of Roslyn is situated directly over the main shaft of the No. 4 mine. Residents reported that the shock of the explosion felt like an earthquake as buildings shook. Had the explosion occurred on a weekday, at least 400 miners would have perished. The photograph above is of a postcard mass produced the day after the explosion. On the back of the card was written, "This is a card showing it during the explosion. Of course, it looks worse than this to us. There are still four men to be found yet. They are looking for them right along."

On October 10, 1896, the Northwest Improvement Company Store opened its doors. Miners could purchase items from the store on credit. This sounded good, but during weeks when work was scarce, goods were bought on credit and miners could easily become indebted to the company store. Sometimes a miner's entire paycheck would be taken to pay the outstanding bill. Robert Brooks's paycheck (right) shows that after a short workweek of three days' hard work (10- to 12-hour days earning between $6.40 and $7 per day), he owed the company store $7.25 and brought home a whopping $8.43 for the week. Sometimes miners worked only two or three days a week.

Boys under 14 were not allowed to work in the mines. To support their families, many boys lied about their age. In the early days, miners were paid by the ton, and it was not uncommon for children to accompany their fathers down in the mine and spend the day picking up the smaller chunks of coal and loading them into the coal cars.

Frank Badda is pictured in the No. 5 mine. Mining is not for the faint of heart—quarters are close and danger is ever present. Badda places coal on the pan line, which moves it down the line by shaking and drops the coal into a coal car to be taken out of the mine. Notice how the cap piece on the timber is being squeezed. (Courtesy of Johnny Ferro.)

Miners pack and shoot the coal with black powder to open up a new shaft. The coal is brought out of the shaft and loaded on cars. The shaft is timbered for safety. When all the coal has been mined from the shaft, the timbers are weakened and the passage is allowed to close. Without the timbers for support, the ground pushes up and the shaft closes. (Courtesy of John Ferro.)

"Lots of guys thought they wanted to work the mines—until they went over the hump and down into the dark," explained John Ferro. "Many times I'd take guys down and bring them right back up. They couldn't stand the thought of the earth above them and didn't even make it off the mancar." Pictured is Johnny Briski on the gravity feed in the No 3 mine. (Courtesy of John Ferro.)

Wash day was a chore for miners' wives. It was common in those days to wash clothes by boiling them in a copper pot on the stove. The last load would be the miner's clothes, which took three (or more) changes of water to get clean. Men came home from the mines covered in black coal dust—the only thing visible were the whites of their eyes.

An old muleskinner was an amateur ventriloquist. His partner, a young kid, was driving a mule that refused to pull. The ventriloquist threw his voice so it sounded like the mule was talking, "It's too heavy. I can't pull it." The scared boy replied to the mule, "When you do decide to pull this load I won't be here to see it," and he ran out of the mine.

Roslyn was a pretty wild town back in the late 1800s. One night, two boys got hold of a stick of dynamite and decided to play a joke. They lit the dynamite, and with sparks flying from the fuse, threw it through the doors of a local tavern. The boys rolled on the ground laughing when they heard an old miner exclaim, "Annabelle!"—slang for Monobel-brand dynamite. Upon hearing this and seeing the blazing stick of dynamite, tavern patrons began to dive through the glass windows and out the doors. As the miners rolled, ran, and flew out of the tavern, the boys were discovered and got their hides tanned. By some miracle, the fuse fizzled and the dynamite did not go off.

Every three months, the links between the coal cars had to be checked for cracks. This was done by taking the links, placing them in a forge and heating them until they were red-hot, which would reveal any cracks. If a link showed signs of stress, it was replaced immediately. (Courtesy of John Ferro.)

Herb Newman (first row, second from right), mine foreman and captain of the Mine Rescue Team, which took home numerous honors over the years, was killed in a freak accident when his crew was drilling and blasting in the mine and a piece of coal ricocheted against a wall and hit Newman in the head. After this accident, miners were required to wear hard hats in the mine.

Four

CULTURAL MELTING POT

Many immigrants came directly to Roslyn from their native lands to work the coal mines. The result was 24 nationalities working together in the mines, rubbing elbows in saloons, praying together in church, and settling arguments with fists when tempers flared.

By 1890, all ethnic groups were tightly organized into lodges and fraternal organizations. Each was proud of their heritage from the old country and took measures to preserve it. The organizations came about to foster companionship and provide insurance and death benefits because the miners received none. At one time, 24 lodges existed in Roslyn—one for each nationality. There were 24 sections in the Roslyn Cemetery—one for each lodge. There were also 24 different sections of town and 24 taverns, each patronized by different nationalities.

Zealous propaganda was whipped up during World War II calling for all nationalities to speak English. It was believed by some in power that people speaking in foreign tongues were most likely plotting against the U.S. government. This attitude was even so in the small town of Roslyn. At the outbreak of World War II, Jim Bardesono, owner of the German Bakery, was asked to change the name of his bakery because of anti-German sentiment among patriotic Americans. Bardesono happily complied, but the new name didn't stick and community members continued to call it the German Bakery, as it is remembered to this day.

There were many accidents and much loss of life in the mines. Tragedy brings people together across racial and ethnic barriers. Each culture retained its unique qualities, but all lived and played and mourned and celebrated together in the same small community.

Olivia Chapetta's brother Ivo Lupis-Vukic traveled to Roslyn from Croatia in 1927 to visit his sister, whom he had not seen for 26 years. Vukic wrote, "Such is frequently the immigrant's fate in life. . . . decades pass before you cross paths and become reacquainted with those who are closest and dearest to you." Upon his departure, Vukic recalled, "The train was coming. I could hear the roar of the engine. My sister begged me to stay. My heart ached as it had never ached before. In just a couple of minutes I would be pulling away from these dear people and would not be stopping until there was a frightening distance between us. I gasped from deep within. Will I ever see you or will you ever see me again." Olivia and her husband, Ivan, lay in this unmarked grave. According to Ivo's memoirs, he and Olivia never saw each other again. (Courtesy of Jay DeBoer.)

Sunday picnics were some of Frank Barich's fondest memories: "The ethnic picnics were a ball. Each nationality had a special location along the riverbank starting at Bull Frog Bridge. The music was great. These picnics were a place to enjoy the company of friends and family. The picnics would often last from daylight to dark." This picture was taken at a 1909 Italian gathering. During the summer, families gathered to sing songs, dance, and eat together. Sometimes there would be a pig roast, and the children would spend their time playing and swimming together.

"As soon as weather permitted the Italians would get together to play Bocce Ball. These games were very precise—measured to a fraction of an inch. Sometimes there were heated arguments," remembers Katie Dalle Kladnik. The Italian men on Fourth Street played bocce ball on a court they built. Bocce games were also played in the alley behind Pete Casazza's store. (Courtesy of Ellensburg Library.)

George Perpich and his girls (from left to right) Mary, Ann, and Dora pose in 1921. Perpich was a cement mason by trade. He did much of the early cement work in the Roslyn Cemetery, which has lasted for nearly a century.

The Hiawatha Council was chartered in Roslyn in 1898. The Red Man Lodge was the men's counterpart. The order was organized to preserve American traditions and provide life insurance and burial benefits to its members. The official garb was moccasins, feather headdress, and full buckskin suits for the men and buckskin dresses and moccasins for the women. Dues to be a member were 10¢ a month or $1.20 per year. Amanda Garnes of Roslyn, standing above in the fringed dress, was the first Great Pocahontas of the State of Washington.

This 1923 photograph of Roslyn Elementary students represents children from 24 nationalities. The children were not listed on the photograph in order of appearance. Pictured are Nellie Henry, Elizabeth Menghal, Emily Ash, Berth Powers, Mary ?, Josephine Genoski, Dora Fera, Vera Erikson, Angeline ?, Trisa Briskey, Lillian Brookhouse, Mary Lewis, Gladys Taylor, Mary Drako, Mayville Bone, Cathrine Boyden, Minnie Bardesono, Tony Blazina, ? Kutchin, William Bennett, Howard Genoski, ? Boone, Patz Pasquan, James MacDonald, Wilbur Munger, Savie Trucano, Rees Thomas, David Owen, Slava Broysovich, Bennie Wezagard, Mike Kussic, Adolph Beramint, John Pickering, John Cornwell, Clinton Gallaher, ? Loby (teacher), and Paul Harper. Four of the children are unidentified.

Maggie and Thomas Thomas's parents were from Scotland. They brought with them the custom of "first footing," which became a New Year's tradition in Roslyn. First Footers went from house to house after midnight to welcome the New Year. Legend said that the first person to cross your threshold after midnight would have an impact on your life in the next year. At each house, folks would visit and drink and eat.

Strong ties were maintained between individuals of common culture and language. Fraternal lodges flourished in Roslyn and contributed to preserving the separate identities of the numerous ethnic groups. The Fraternal Order of Knights of Pythias and its members (pictured here) were dedicated to the cause of universal peace.

United States of America.

Territory of Washington,

Fourth Judicial District.

I, *Giuseppe Musso* do declare on oath that it is bona fide my intention to become a citizen of the UNITED STATES OF AMERICA, that I will support the Constitution of the United States of America, the Organic Act and Laws of Washington Territory, and renounce forever all allegiance and fidelity to all and every foreign Prince, Potentate, State and Sovereignty whatever, and particularly to *Umbert King of Italy* whose subject I was. So help me God.

Giuseppe Musso

Subscribed and sworn to before me, this *29th* day of *June* A. D. 188*8*.

W. H. Peterson
Clerk.

By .... Deputy.

I, *W. H. Peterson* Clerk of the District Court of the Fourth Judicial District, Washington Territory, hereby certify that the above is a true copy of the Declaration of Intention of *Giuseppe Musso* to become a citizen of the United States, as the same appears of record in my office.

Witness my hand and the Seal of the said Court, at *Ellensburgh, W.T.* this *29th* day of *June* A. D. 188*8*.

W. H. Peterson
Clerk.

Guiseppe Musso was the father of Frank Musso, founder of the Roslyn Museum (see page 35). According to letters found, Guiseppe Musso worked hard to prepare and took great pride in becoming a U.S. citizen. "I, Guiseppe Musso, do declare on oath that it is bona fide my intention to become a citizen of the United States of America, that I will support the Constitution of the United States of America, the Organic Acts and Laws of the Washington Territory and renounce forever all allegiance and fidelity to all and every foreign Prince, Potentate, State and Sovereignty whatever and particularly to the King of Italy whose subject I was. So help me God. Subscribed and Sworn this 29th Day of June 1888."

Attracted by reports of great economic opportunities, immigrants from many countries flocked to Roslyn to work the mines. At night, they attended citizenship school at the YMCA (above) in order to become U.S. citizens. Helene Leniski remembers when her grandmother took citizenship classes and how she was so proud to be studying to become an American citizen. After her grandmother died, Helene was going through some of her belongings and found the notebook she used during citizenship classes. One of the questions and answers on the test was as follows: (Q) Vat iz da republic reprezentiv form of govermenit? (A) Konstentushin of U.S. Suprimi lay of da U.S. This shows how difficult and challenging a time the immigrants had with the language.

In the mid-1800s, Chinese immigrants came to the Pacific Northwest to work the mines and build the railroad. White workers resented the starvation wages and intolerable conditions the Chinese were willing to endure. Chinese immigrants undercut local labor, and because of this, they faced discrimination, acts of violence, riots, and even murder. In 1887, twenty-five Chinese miners living at China Camp just above Roslyn were murdered by a mob of white men.

Blasius ("Blas") Javornik was a trapper and game hunter who lived in Roslyn. He made his living selling pelts and was an accomplished taxidermist. Blas spent his days trekking all over the Cascades hunting and checking his traps. He lived an adventurous life and had the wild game (including a gorilla) on his wall to prove it. Locals remember that Blas's walls were covered with animals he had hunted and stuffed.

Thomas Petrich and his wife, Pauline, came to Roslyn from Croatia. They had six children. On the day baby Phyllis (seated on her mother's lap) was born, her eight-year-old brother, Slavel, was playing with a neighbor and found a loaded gun. The boys were looking at the gun when it went off, shooting Slavel and killing him. Pictured in 1909 are, from left to right (first row) Phyllis (baby), Pauline, Thomas, and Alvina; (second row) Julian, Marian, and Frank.

The Cusworth family emigrated from England to Roslyn in 1890, enticed by stories of making a good living in the coal mines. In 1892, Joseph Cusworth Sr. and Joseph Cusworth Jr. were killed in a mine explosion. Pictured in 1906 are, from left to right, Dave, Vera, Lorena, mother Maud, and baby Frances Cusworth. Dave and Vera both had the mumps. Frances was born in this house, which is located across from the Catholic church.

Many families made wine. The Bounadi family, who lived at 16 Fifth Street, was no exception. During Prohibition, it was illegal to make wine, so when the inspector came into town, the wine had to be hidden. Turns out the pigpen was a great place to hide bottles of wine. The downside was after the inspector left . . . all the bottles had to be washed.

Food was an important part of family tradition—and especially so during a wedding. "It's a Yugoslav custom for the boys to work all night to get the pig ready and the fire just so. While the men were busy with the pig roast, the women would bake a Yugoslavian nut roll," remembers Veda Huchnit. According to tradition, the nut roll was shared by the Brozovich couple during their ceremony to bring them prosperity and a long, happy life together.

Ida Mason of Roslyn lived to be over 100 and told captivating stories of her childhood: "Each summer our tribe we go Salmon La Sac. The men they fish and the women make baskets and the children pick huckleberries. The baskets made from bark and roots of white cedar which grow only on Stampede Pass. The old ways, all our people, all our friends, all gone now . . . long gone, nobody left but me." The CD of memories was made through a grant as a history project and is out of print. (Courtesy of Traci Giles.)

The Seresun family came to Roslyn from Czechoslovakia in the late 1800s. The family owned a grocery store in what is now the barbershop just up from city hall. The store was called Seresun Shur-Fine Grocery. Pictured are, from left to right, (first row) Mother Seresun and Andy; (second row) Mr. Seresun, Mike, Mary, and Pete.

Camilla Saivetto is remembered as quite a character. One year, when work was scarce, Camilla came up with a plan. Her husband said, "No boarders!" Instead, she decided to wash clothes for extra money. But she didn't have a washing machine, so she sent a letter and a down payment of $5 to Sears and they shipped her a machine. Camilla recalled, "I was so tickled then I thought, 'Now I wonder how to run this thing!'" (Courtesy of Jay DeBoer.)

The Odd Fellows Lodge originated in England in the 1700s and followed immigrants to America. The Odd Fellows was set up to care for its member families during times when there were no unions or health organizations. Their goal was to offer help when members needed it. The Odd Fellows' Band played in parades and local celebrations, and lodge members are buried in their own section of the Roslyn Cemetery.

Five

ROSLYN'S BLACK HISTORY

In 1888, Roslyn miners went on strike, demanding safer working conditions, better pay, and an eight-hour workday. The Knights of Labor represented the miners, but Northern Pacific refused to recognize the union or bargain with the miners. Instead of negotiating, the mining company decided to break the strike, bringing in 400 blacks by cattle car from the East and the South and filled the jobs of striking white miners with blacks. Many of the blacks who migrated had been former slaves.

James Shepperson, a labor recruiter, was sent by the railroad to find people with the motivation to relocate. The black miners were not told by Shepperson that they were being taken to Roslyn as strikebreakers.

It became apparent to the black miners there was trouble down the line when Pinkerton guards boarded the cattle cars in Missoula, Montana, and handed out guns to the passengers. At that point, the black miners were told they would be strikebreakers. They had no home to go to and realized what awaited them was no worse than what they left behind.

When the train arrived in Roslyn, angry miners lined the tracks and the guards on the train had guns pointed out each opening to discourage violence. Unable to stop in Roslyn, the train continued on to Ronald, where the black miners were heavily guarded. The next morning, under heavy guard, they were taken to the mines to begin work. For the protection of the black miners, who were willing to work longer hours and for less money than the whites, the mine was fortified with dirt barriers, logs, and barbed wire.

When the strike was over, blacks were kept on in the mines. Mining in those days was difficult and dangerous work that required cooperation among miners. In this environment, mutual respect began to develop. Tensions eased in time as both blacks and whites began working together in the mines.

As time passed, black miners became a part of Roslyn's community—building homes, businesses, churches, and community organizations. For two years after the strike, the black population in Roslyn outnumbered whites.

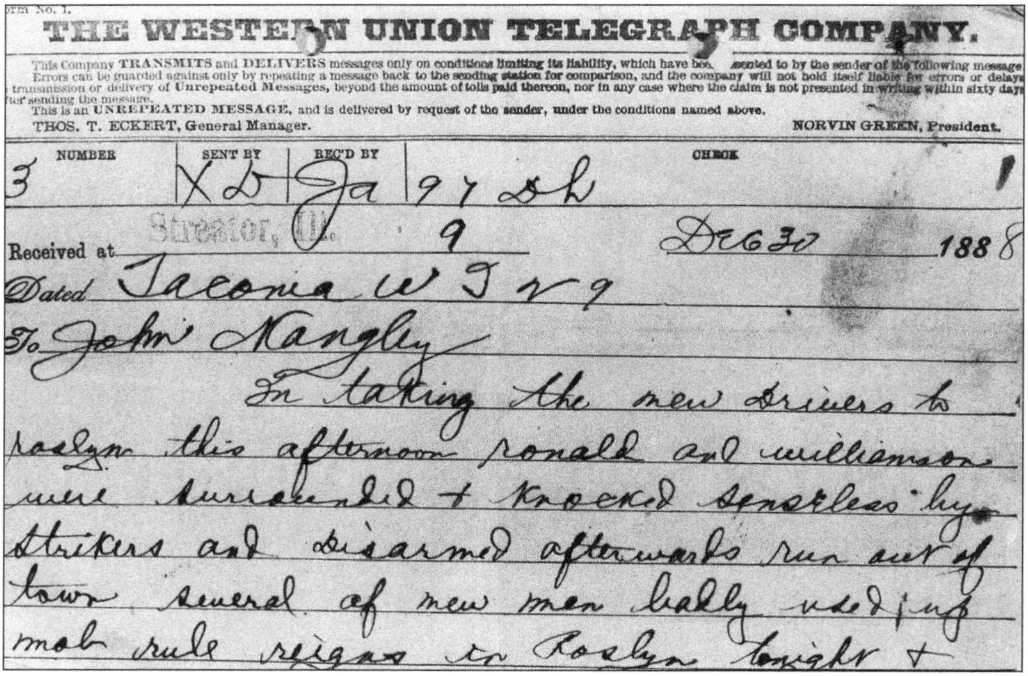

Form No. 1.

THE WESTERN UNION TELEGRAPH COMPANY.

This Company TRANSMITS and DELIVERS messages only on conditions limiting its liability, which have been assented to by the sender of the following message. Errors can be guarded against only by repeating a message back to the sending station for comparison, and the company will not hold itself liable for errors or delays in transmission or delivery of Unrepeated Messages, beyond the amount of tolls paid thereon, nor in any case where the claim is not presented in writing within sixty days after sending the message.

This is an UNREPEATED MESSAGE, and is delivered by request of the sender, under the conditions named above.

THOS. T. ECKERT, General Manager. NORVIN GREEN, President.

NUMBER	SENT BY	REC'D BY		CHECK
3	XD	Ja	97 DH	1

Received at Streator, Ill. 9 Dec 30 1888

Dated Tacoma W T 29

To John Mangley

In taking the new drivers to roslyn this afternoon ronald and williamson were surrounded & knocked senseless by strikers and disarmed afterwards run out of town several of new men badly used up mob rule reigns in Roslyn tonight &

This December 30, 1888, telegram reads: "In taking the new drivers to Roslyn this afternoon Ronald and Williamson were surrounded and knocked senseless by strikers and disarmed. Afterwards run out of town. Several of new men badly used up. Mob rule reigns in Roslyn tonight and deputy sheriffs and guards were also run out of town by strikers and I have wired territorial governor regarding situation and asked his immediate assistance to protect us. Sheriff has not responded to our calls. Property at Roslyn has no protection tonight." (Courtesy of Ellensburg Public Library.)

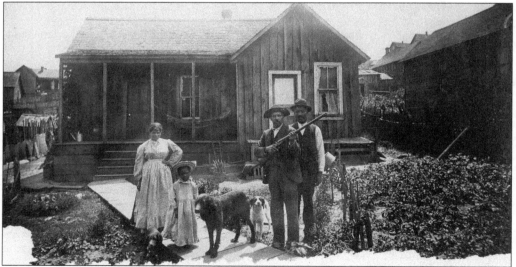

Guns were carried by the original black settlers and miners in Roslyn, as tensions often ran high in the early days between blacks and whites. Violence was not uncommon among the striking white miners and the strikebreaking blacks. The man on the left is wearing a gun belt and holding a rifle. White miners referred to the black strikebreakers as "The Curse of the 400."

Samuel T. Packwood and his wife, Margaret Holmes Packwood, were early pioneers in Kittitas County. Packwood was the county sheriff during the strike of 1888 and was often called to Roslyn to keep law and order during a time of explosive relations between striking miners and the newly arrived black strikebreakers. (Courtesy of Ellensburg Public Library.)

During the strike, black miners were threatened and assaulted and got in the habit of carrying the guns given to them by the Pinkerton guards. They went to work armed and came home armed. The man on the left wearing a gun belt and carrying a gun is Grandpa Sport. Ethel Craven cared for him when he was elderly, and his gun and gun belt were left to the Craven family and later passed down to Willie Craven (Washington State's first black mayor).

Big Jim Shepperson was a labor recruiter hired by Northern Pacific to bring blacks in to break the 1888 strike. Shep did not tell the miners he recruited they had been hired as strikebreakers. Shepperson also owned a social club for blacks in Roslyn. He became a negotiator with the mine bosses and an early spokesman for the black community in Roslyn. (Courtesy of Ellensburg Public Library.)

In August 1888, Alexander Ronald, superintendent of mines, was sitting in his living room when he heard the cry, "Here he is boys, let's get him!" Ronald was dragged from his home by an angry mob of striking miners, beaten unconscious, and tied to the train tracks because the miners felt he was responsible for the company's refusal to accept their terms. The conductor on an approaching train thought Ronald's body was brush on the tracks until the train got closer, at which point he said, "My God, it's a man on the tracks and we can't stop!" He pulled the brakes, but the train was on a downgrade into Roslyn with a string of heavily loaded coal cars behind it. The train's fireman jumped from the moving train, ran ahead, untied Ronald and pulled him from the tracks just as the train passed over the spot where he had been tied.

Lucy Breckenridge was born into slavery in Stanton, Virginia, in 1855. Lucy's husband, Henry Breckenridge, came to Roslyn in 1888 to break the strike. In 1989, Lucy was recognized by the Washington State Genealogical Society as one of the first black citizens to have settled in Washington.

This couple, photographed on their wedding day in 1892, shows the status afforded to African American residents of Roslyn. Employment in Roslyn brought blacks, many former slaves, a social status they had not experienced before. The mines supported them and their families. The kind of personal protection offered by the armed guards was dignifying, and blacks' earning power was comparable to that of whites. (Courtesy of Ellensburg Public Library.)

Mary Perkins was the sister of Henry Breckenridge. Mary was also born into slavery on the same plantation as her brother Henry and his wife, Lucy. Henry came to Roslyn first, and Lucy and Mary later followed. Mary owned a store in Roslyn for many years. Roslyn residents of different races and nationalities each had their own stores and taverns and tended to cater to those establishments. In the photograph below, Mary Perkins and her family enjoy a picnic.

Harriet Jackson Williams (pictured around 1924), Ethel Craven's mother, came from Braidwood, Illinois, to Roslyn in September 1888. Harriet was born in Richmond, Virginia, in 1871 and journeyed with other wives and families of migrating miners to Roslyn to be reunited with their husbands. Harriet Williams and her husband owned several large farms around Grandview, Washington. She died in 1926. (Courtesy of Ellensburg Public Library.)

Ethel Craven was born in Roslyn in 1906. She remembers that as a child she would "go up a tree like a squirrel. Folks would be talking under me and I'd hear everything they'd say. They didn't know I was up in that tree and I'd go home and tell momma what was gonna happen." (Courtesy of Ellensburg Public Library.)

Ethel (1906–1993) and Samuel (1895–1969) Craven are on the porch of their Roslyn home. They had 13 children together. The Cravens are the last remaining family of the original black pioneers who came to Roslyn during the strike of 1888 and were among the first black settlers of Washington State. (Courtesy of Ellensburg Public Library.)

Leola Mae McClain, pictured in 1923 at one year old, was the daughter of Ethel Williams Craven. Leola May married and moved to Seattle, where she became active in various community and civil organizations. In 1976, Jesse Jackson presented Leola Mae with the Martin Luther King Humanitarian Award for outstanding leadership in the black community. (Courtesy of Ellensburg Public Library.)

Samuel Craven, pictured on his 45th wedding anniversary to Ethel, moved to Roslyn from Texas in 1922 and worked in the Nos. 3, 4, 5, and 7 mines until he retired in 1961. Ethel Craven recalled, "One day my husband Samuel and his brother came home crying like babies because a block of coal fell on a man and crushed him and there was nothing they could do except watch him die." (Courtesy of Ellensburg Public Library.)

Ethel Craven was named Kittitas County Mother of the Year in 1970, and in 1985 became the first Afro American Pioneer Queen in Kittitas County. Pioneer Days are held each year to celebrate Roslyn's pioneers—where they came from, their cultural roots, their joys and sorrows, and what they found in the Washington Territory. (Courtesy of Ellensburg Public Library.)

Willie Craven, son of Samuel and Ethel Craven, was elected mayor of Roslyn in 1975, becoming Washington State's first black mayor. When Willie was elected, he told reporters, "I didn't run for this job as a black man, but as a man. I wanted an equal chance to try." Looking back, Willie remembers the most rewarding part of the job was "helping the people."

Wesley Craven, son of Samuel and Ethel Craven, was a Golden Gloves welterweight and heavyweight champion boxer. Wesley became a professional boxer, but his career was cut short by a serious eye injury. (Courtesy of Ellensburg Public Library.)

On July 10, 2001, Tom Craven, a firefighter for the U.S. Forest Service, was called to fight a fire that was later determined to have been started by an abandoned campfire. Willie Craven, Tom's father, remembered, "Tom was told the fire was under control. But while he and his crew were mopping up, the wind changed and they had no idea the fire was coming their way. One firefighter survived to tell us what a hero Tom had been. Tom sensed something was wrong and went up a hill for a look around. He ran back down the hill and said, 'We've got to get out of here, the fire's coming.' But there was no escape. The fire had them boxed in and they didn't have a chance. When my boy died, the town shut down for his funeral. People lined the streets and saluted him. It meant the world to me. Me and my brothers built Tom's memorial in the Roslyn Cemetery. The rock and trees came from the place where he died." For information on the Thirtymile Fire Memorial built by the U.S. Forest Service in memory of Tom Craven and his crew, please visit www.fs.fed.us/r6/wenatchee/fire/thirtymile/thirtymile-brochure.pdf. (Courtesy of Jay DeBoer.)

Powell Barnett Sr. was born a slave in Virginia in 1855 and was one of the original African American miners who arrived in Roslyn, Washington Territory, in 1888. Barnett with his wife and children played an active role in Roslyn's African American community. (Courtesy of Ellensburg Public Library.)

This was the homestead of Cynthia (Mrs. William) Barnett, who was born in 1888 in Louisiana and moved to Roslyn in the early 1900s. Also pictured are Cynthia's two sons: Stanchol "Stan," born 1915 (left), and William, born 1911. Mining was hard, dirty, and dangerous work. Many blacks quit the mines to homestead.

Powell S. Barnett (1883–1971) grew up in Roslyn, where he mined coal and played in a local band. He moved to Seattle in 1906. Barnett broke color barriers in the all-white Musician's Union. He is pictured here in 1908 with a member of the Volunteers of America Band. He was active in integration and racial harmony. A park in Seattle was named for Barnett. (Courtesy of Ellensburg Public Library.)

Brothers Powell N. Barnett (rear) and Johnny were the sons of musician Powell S. Barnett Jr., who moved from Roslyn to Seattle in 1906. The boys enjoyed returning to Roslyn to visit family. (Courtesy of Ellensburg Public Library.)

Payne's Military Band (pictured *c.* 1920) performed at a variety of social events in Roslyn. Making music and playing at social events, black and white, demonstrated the lack of racial tensions among blacks and whites in Roslyn in later years. (Courtesy of Ellensburg Public Library.)

Arthur Wiseker attended Roslyn schools with his brothers and sisters. He later became a track star at the University of Minnesota, where this picture was taken in 1929. Arthur set track records that were unbroken until the late 1980s. (Courtesy of Ellensburg Public Library.)

The black citizens of Roslyn built up the Black People's Church. The church was the center of Roslyn's black community and sponsored events such as plays, Bible study, suppers, and holiday programs. On warm Sunday mornings when the church doors were open, Preacher Brown could be heard giving his sermon a block away. The anomaly in this photograph was analyzed by Jay DeBoer, technical director of Washington State Paranormal Investigations and Research. His analysis and explanation were lengthy and can be viewed in detail at www.wspir.com.

Six

TOWN OF REMARKABLE CHARACTERS

There was never a photograph to show Andy Vlahovich and Frank Elenich's Model T pickup—the one they owned for half an hour. But as Frank tells the story in "Old Country to Coal Country," you'll feel you are along for the ride:

> In 1939, Andy Vlahovich (age 15) and, me, Frank Elenich (age 11) decided to go in partners on a Motel T pickup truck. We were told it was ours for the taking so we headed up the ridge to go get it. When we spotted our Model T it wasn't quite what we expected—it was in two sections—the front section sat about 50 feet from the back section—and there was no motor.
>
> We pieced the two sections together with baling wire. We also attached a piece of baling wire to the rear wheel brakes so we could pull it and slow down when needed. Then we pushed the pickup over to the edge of a hill. The truck we were about to ride in was held together with baling wire, had a seat but no floorboards, no windshield, no motor and no transmission. Andy and me jumped in and off we went.
>
> As we were blazing down the hill Andy, who was driving, yelled at me to pull up on the brakes. I grabbed the bailing wire and pulled...and nothing. In the mix I dropped the brake wire (not that it mattered) and the truck was freewheeling down the incline. To try and slow the truck down, Andy steered into a high bank and the rig tipped up on two wheels and the front fenders and cowling fell off (held on only by baling wire) and were dragging on the ground—which slowed the truck down just a bit before it ran into a pine tree and threw us both out in the bushes.
>
> We got up, stood back, looked at our wrecked Model T and felt very lucky to have survived. What we were most proud of though is that we were truck owners for about a half an hour.

Luke McCook, a gentleman of the railways, was a man of many talents. During the Depression, Luke came to Roslyn each summer by railroad car after wintering in California. Luke was an expert at fixing household items and was willing to work for a hot meal. Many houses in Roslyn still have repairs in them made by Luke. He spent his summers going from household to household repairing items. In the evening, youngsters would gather around Luke's campfire to listen to his stories. He had endless tales to spin. One summer in the late 1940s, Luke did not return to Roslyn. He was greatly missed and to this day is fondly remembered by locals in Roslyn.

For men, a trip to the barbershop was a men-only social affair. At the barbershop, men could talk men stuff and safely tell off-color jokes. They could yell, swear, scratch, and have a good old time. Life was good in the barbershops of yesteryear.

From left to right, Mrs. Hopkins, Mrs. Morgan, Mrs. Snyder, and Mrs. Tasche are very amused. The two children are not—having just been chased to the safety of their mothers' arms by a pack of geese. Not only did the Morgan family have roosters that would fly over the fence and peck you in the head, they had geese that would chase you like they were junkyard dogs.

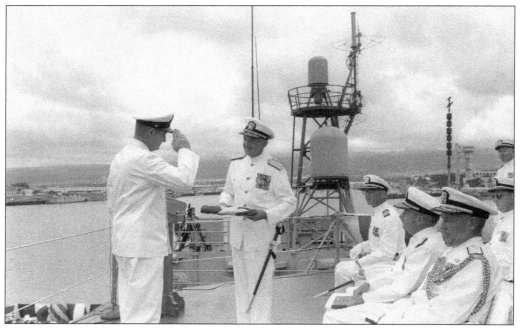

Adm. John H. Sides, commander in chief of the Pacific Fleet, accepted his flag after it was lowered from the mainmast of the USS *Topeka* (CLG-8) on September 30, 1963, signifying the end of his naval career. Admiral Sides, a native of Roslyn, was involved in developing robot planes for use in combat. Each robot plane was armed with a 2,000-pound bomb, so accuracy in hitting intended targets was crucial.

Riding herd can be dangerous business for cowboys . . . especially when doing so in Converse tennis shoes, bareback, with no reins, and on a cow wearing a lei, a crown of flowers, and a tail ribbon. This little buckaroo was an amazing cowboy because keeping his seat on a bony cow while swinging a lasso would have been hard to do.

Tony Bailey (center) had a secret. In 1949, she worked for 11 months alongside the other miners without betraying his (or rather her) secret. Tony went so far as to take out several Roslyn women on dates without them ever knowing he was a she and her real name was Gloria. Gloria messed up one evening while out on the town by absentmindedly entering the women's bathroom dressed as a man. The gig was up when an off-duty sheriff spotted her coming out of the bathroom and arrested her. Gloria was ambitious and came up with the idea to work in the mines to raise money to buy a restaurant. After she was found out, she sold her story to a newspaper reporter to further add to her savings.

There were some unusual people who worked in the mines. One in particular was an Italian miner named Riela, who would work all day in the mines, go home, and dress up as a woman before coming back to the taverns for a night of fun. There are no details about what kind of fun he had in mind, but Roslyn was a wild mining town in the late 1800s, and most likely, he found whatever fun he was looking for.

On July 18, 1914, the circus rolled into town. Tents were set up on Pennsylvania Avenue. During the show, a snake charmer named Myrtle Wilson was bitten by a rattlesnake. Dr. Newgard tried to save Myrtle, but she died that night. Her husband (also a member of the circus) was to come back for her but never did. Myrtle is buried in the Old City Cemetery. (Courtesy of Jay DeBoer.)

These young ladies were all dressed up in their finest and heading out to a neighborhood tea party. With parasol, purse, and shawl, the tea party set never looked so sharp. There is no record of who these adorable little girls are, but bets are their tea party was a hit.

Roslyn used to have an 8:00 p.m. curfew whistle that meant all kids had to be off the streets and at home. Child rearing in those days was straightforward and uncomplicated. If a kid was disciplined at school, they would be in for it at home. If they got in trouble downtown, there would be more trouble when they got home. Pictured is one mother a kid would be wise not to tangle with.

Sharon Roletto Browning remembers, "When I was a little girl my grandmother Lena Roletto's Italian lady friends Minnie, Maggie, Bina, Mary and Tunietta would get together to celebrate each other's birthdays with an afternoon of card playing, visiting and good treats. My grandmother would sometimes take me along." Author Note: The women in this photo from Roslyn's archives could not be identified.

Tom Bryant and his bear cub, BoBo, were a big hit with Roslyn residents. The bear cub would hibernate all winter, then come spring, Tom would hone the bear's skills and bring him to town to perform tricks for the townsfolk. BoBo and Tom earned enough money each summer that they both could hibernate for the long, cold winters.

Ethel Saxby recalls, "One of my best students kept falling asleep in class. I couldn't figure out why all the children in the room giggled when I asked if he was going to bed early enough. Come to find out, the boy's family was the first in the mining camp to get a radio and all the neighbors would gather each evening to listen and the boy couldn't go to sleep until late when the power was shut off for the night and the neighbors went home."

Dorothy Sharp, an operator for the Roslyn Telephone Company, spent her days wearing headphones in front of a console that contained hundred of holes. Every few seconds, there would be a buzzing sound and one of the holes would glow red. Dorothy plugged a cord in the glowing hole and answered, "Hello, Operator." Then she plugged the other end of the cord into another hole to ring the party being called.

Bootlegging was a booming operation in Roslyn and Ronald in the 1920s. The still in Ronald was by far the biggest in the state. It was located underground and connected by a series of underground tunnels to the bootleggers' garages. On August 18, 1928, there were 128 barrels of "White Mule" moonshine stored down there. When the still exploded, flames shot 40 feet in the air and sent a fireball down through the tunnel system. Bert (Old Man) Pelligrini was in the still room at the time of the explosion. He climbed out of the tunnel on fire, and his wife tried to put him out with a garden hose. He died later that night from his burns. It took 24 hours to bring the fire under control, and 80 acres of forest burned. Dante Panieri recalled, "People came with pitchers, pails, dishpans and even bedpans to fill with the "White Mule" moonshine. No one seemed to mind the charred bits of wood and ashes floating in it." One Ronald resident commented, "Half the town was burned and the other half was drunk."

Tony Walkovich was a longshoreman from Italy before coming to America. Tony operated a tavern on Pennsylvania Avenue. His nephew Richard Hayes remembered one Fourth of July: "The tavern doors were wide open as the parade went past and a thirsty rider rode his horse into the tavern and ordered a beer. My uncle served him and he gulped his beer down from the saddle. My Uncle Tony was loud and opinionated. He had a tendency to get angry, slam his hand down on the bar making the beer glasses jump and exclaim in broken English, 'Datsa da boolsheets!'" (Courtesy of Jay DeBoer.)

During the Depression, Mexican JoJo sold tamales to miners at lunch and at all-night card games in Roslyn taverns. Tavern owners loved him because the spicy tamales made the gamblers thirsty. He was asked, but never told, his secret ingredient. One day, JoJo left town. Imagine locals' surprise when they showed up to check on JoJo and found barrels of cat hides and cat carcasses in his yard. (Courtesy of Jay DeBoer.)

Residents from several of Roslyn's 24 ethnic neighborhoods came together to form a band. There was no money for members to purchase instruments, so they borrowed them from the local American Legion and the Veterans of the Foreign Wars. This band, formed from many different cultures, made beautiful music and played in many a parade.

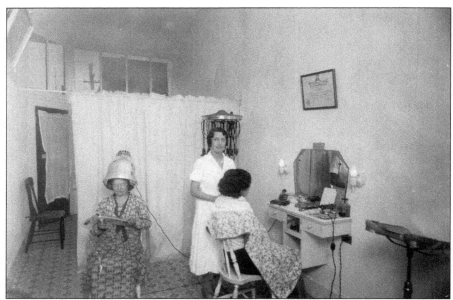

Giolitta "Jean" Camerlo Pasin operated Jean's Beauty Shoppe from September 1931 to September 1937 in a remodeled section of her mother's hardware store. The permanent wave machine with electrical wires dangling down (looking more like battery clamps than something a woman would put in her hair) was purchased from Howe Beauty Supply in October 1931 and was used until 1970, when parts for it were no longer available. Jean's mother, Mrs. Giono, is sitting under the dryer, and Jean is styling the hair of her childhood friend, Anne Katcher Bogachus.

Jean's Beauty Shoppe

PERMANENT WAVES

$2.25 and $3.95

Marcel 75c
Finger Wave ... 50c

Call 91 or 575   Roslyn

Seven

CELEBRATIONS AND PASTIMES

Time and again, those who grew up in Roslyn refer to the simple, uncomplicated, and wonderful time their childhood years were. Most children came from families with little money, but they had the richness of everything in life that mattered—love, kindness, family, and friends.

Celebrations like Fourth of July and Labor Day were days kids looked forward to all year because there were parades and picnics in the park. On May Day, children made paper baskets and filled them with wildflowers (curly heads, buttercups, and daisies), then hung them on people's doorknobs. On New Year's Day, kids went from house to house with an apple and people would stick coins in it for good luck after being wished a Happy New Year. (Courtesy of "Old Country to Coal Country")

Angie Mrak Briski recalled:

As kids we spent hours jumping rope downtown and playing hopscotch and Run Sheepie Run. We threw rocks at bats under the streetlights, sometimes not hitting the bats, but the streetlights instead. Wintertime was spent sledding and we always had a bonfire compliments of the greased rags from Northern Pacific coal cars. Many a summer night we used to sit on the porch and be entertained with accordion and piano music. Everything we had was homemade. Jello was a treat we enjoyed only in the winter when mother put it in the snow to set. Sometimes we'd get a few pennies for penny candy. That was a treat. Life was simple, but it was fun.

Baseball was a popular pastime in Roslyn. The above photograph of the Roslyn Grays was taken in 1904. There were several teams that formed the Roslyn League. The first teams to play in the late 1800s were known as the Whiskey Bottle Team, the Pop Bottle Team, and the First Team. Willie Craven reminisces, "When we were kids we loved the job of baseball shagger. It was hard to come by baseballs back then and teams didn't want to lose any so they'd hire us kids to chase out of bounds balls for 25 cents a game. Sometimes the balls would go in the pond and we'd go in after them. More often that not, we'd run across garter snakes in there. Boy, we'd hear the crack of that bat and if the ball flew out of bounds, we were gone."

Jimmy Claxton (1895–1940), a baseball legend from Roslyn, has often been compared to Satchel Paige. Claxton was a leftie who threw a blazing fastball and a mean curveball. He struck out batter after batter and was a consistent hitter. Claxton was light skinned and green eyed with black hair and passed himself off as a Native American named Chief Yellow Horse so he could play in the majors. No blacks were allowed in the majors in those days. He played for the Cleveland Indians, but when it was found out he had "colored blood," despite how talented he was, he was dropped from the majors. Saxton would start his pitching windup while facing second base, not home plate. Then he would windmill his southpaw pitching arm once, twice, or three times; pivot on his left foot; kick his right leg high in the air (over his head); and let loose with a fastball, a curveball, or a drop ball. He had amazing control of the ball and was a true baseball legend.

Each Fourth of July, there was a grand celebration in Roslyn. The big attraction was the Liberty Wagon, with Uncle Sam, Miss Liberty, and 48 little girls dressed up in white waving flags. The festivities continued on through the day with sack races, an obstacle course, and an old man's race (for men over 50). There was also a bike race, wheelbarrow race, hose race, barrel rolling race, egg toss, and a squaw's footrace of 100 yards. The big day ended with a clay pigeon shooting contest. There were 25 targets, and the top prize was $20. The entrance fee was 50¢.

Anytime the Roslyn Brewery had a Labor Day barbeque and put up a sign that read, "Eat, Drink and Be Merry Free!," the party was bound to be a success. Labor Day 1912 was no exception. The whole town was invited, and the beer flowed freely. People came in their Sunday best to eat, socialize, and drink . . . for free!

John Bardesono (driving the team) came to Roslyn in 1900. He bought the German Bakery from a German man and decided to keep the name. At the outbreak of World War II, Bardesono happily complied with requests to change the name because of anti-German sentiment in America, but the new name didn't stick and community members continued to call it the German Bakery. Bardesono was active in the community, and each year, he entered a float in the Fourth of July parade. Most years, he won first place, and 1914 was no exception. His floats were always decked out with ovens and bakers at work, and freshly baked cookies were handed out to spectators lining the parade route.

Willie Craven remembers, "Roslyn really did Christmas up right for the kids when I was young. Each year the company store would bring in a big tree and it would be decorated with lights and was real pretty in the snow. One evening close to Christmas, the fire truck would start at the top of Town Hill with the siren blaring and slowly make its way down through town. Santa was in the back waving to all the kids. Kids lined up for a long ways back—two lines—one on either side of the fire truck stretching up the mine road. Boy, you couldn't wait to get in that line. Each kid would get an orange or an apple and a big bag of candy. We thought we were in Heaven. It would be cold and usually snowing but we didn't care, we'd stand in that line for hours waiting our turn. Santa was on the back of the fire truck and kids could sit in his lap and tell him what they wanted for Christmas."

Sledding was great fun for the children of Roslyn. There was the long haul up Catholic Hill, then the swift ride to the bottom. If the wind was right, a kid could ride all the way through town to city hall. Willie Craven says, "We'd come blazing off that hill, flying around corners and across streets. Our parents would get after us for that. But oh, what fun we had."

John Donovan and his boys often enjoyed a ride from Roslyn to Lake Cle Elum on their bicycles. The bicycles the Donovans rode were state of the art in 1890 and a great improvement over Penny-Farthing bikes, which weighed about 45 pounds and were dangerous, because if a rider stopped quickly, he could topple over backward.

Roslyn had a dance hall that was popular among the teenage set in the 1920s and 1930s. Dances started at 9:00 p.m. sharp. Boys lined up along one side of the dance hall and girls along the other. The band played nonstop until around 11:30 p.m., when a hat was passed around to collect donations for the band to stay an extra hour—which always happened no matter how much money was collected.

Each spring, various civic groups clean up and decorate the Roslyn Cemetery. Older family members point out headstones of loved ones and tell stories of days gone by. This picture was taken on Memorial Day 1955, and all the graves in the cemetery were decorated with flowers and flags. Family and friends gathered amid the pine trees to remember those who served our country—especially those who made the ultimate sacrifice.

During summer months, camping and fishing was the way many families spent time together. It was not uncommon to pack up and head out in May, setting up camp and keeping the camp all summer. Parents would return to town during the week, and older kids would stay at the campsite all summer long.

In the days before cars, Roslyn Carriage and Wagon Works did a thriving business servicing Roslyn's wagons. Wagons had wheels, brakes, and all manner of floorboards and seats to keep intact. Wagons got flat tires (of sorts), too. There was a forge in the shop for making metal coverings for wooden spoke wheels. Long strips of metal were heated red-hot then shaped to fit the wheels.

The Roslyn Band was popular in parades and at local celebrations. They were a hit with spectators as they marched along playing popular tunes. The band is best remembered for playing at opening ceremonies of baseball games in Roslyn.

Participants in Roslyn's annual Fourth of July parade were directed in the 1899 Grand Celebration Official Program to be at Unity Hall by 9:00 a.m. in order to be assigned places: "The parade will start at 9:30 a.m. sharp and march through town to the Base Ball Grounds where a selection by the Roslyn Band will be played, the Declaration of Independence read, and the Star Spangled Banner sung."

The Fourth of July parade was something kids looked forward to all year. Ray Owen recalled that growing up in Roslyn in the early 1900s was a kid's dream: "Long, warm summer nights, Fourth of July parade and celebration in the park, playing kick the can under the arc lights, building chipmunk traps, the sound of bike tires on the wooden sidewalks and making scooters from old roller skates and orange crates."

Eight

NORTHERN EXPOSURE

Northern Exposure began as an eight-episode summer-replacement series on CBS in 1990. *Northern Exposure* takes a humorous look at life in Cicely—a remote Alaskan town with a population of 215—through the eyes of transplanted New Yorker Dr. Joel Fleishman (Rob Morrow), who ends up in Cicely to practice medicine in exchange for having his medical school bills paid off.

Joel looks at Cicely's eccentric residents with raised eyebrows—as crazy as New York was, he has never seen anything like this before. The townsfolk include Maurice Minnifield (Barry Corbin), an ex-astronaut and the town's millionaire entrepreneur; Maggie O'Connell (Janine Turner), a bush pilot, Dr. Joel's landlady, and reluctant love interest; Chris "In-The-Morning" Stevens (John Corbett), Cicely's existential deejay and clergyman; Holling Vincoeur (John Cullum), a 60-something tavern owner living with the 18-year-old love of his life; Ed Chigliak (Darren Burrows), a slow-talking Native American with an IQ of 180 who learned everything he knows about life from the movies; Shelly Tambo (Cynthia Geary), an 18-year-old beauty pageant winner who dumps Maurice for his best friend Holling; Ruth-Anne Miller (Peg Phillips), a store owner who dispenses advice to residents who shop in her store; and Marilyn Whirlwind (Elaine Miles), Dr. Joel's quirky assistant.

Producers looked in five states and Canada for the perfect Cicely, Alaska. Joshua Brand and John Falsey liked the sound of the name Cicely and were looking for the perfect location to shoot their series. Brand and Falsey happened on Roslyn by accident and fell in love with the town. "It is Cicely," they said.

The show was a huge success and went on to win numerous awards, including several Emmys and Golden Globes. A total of 110 episodes were produced.

The humorously antagonistic relationship between Joel and Maggie was one of *Northern Exposure*'s greatest strengths—due in no small part to the chemistry that existed naturally between the actors. Janine Turner (Maggie) enjoyed her scenes with Rob Morrow (Joel), "I told the writers I wanted more kissing scenes with Joel because I was living vicariously through Maggie."

Northern Exposure crept onto the CBS summer lineup in 1990 almost unnoticed. While airing as a replacement series, *Northern Exposure* picked up a respectable following that quickly turned the show into a hit. Janine Turner was surprised: "I knew when I was doing it that I was working on something that had great class and quality. So we all just kind of kept our fingers crossed, but it's still surprising to me the kind of hard-core cult following we gained." The show went on to be a hit and received numerous awards.

The Running of the Bulls is an annual event in Cicely where all the male residents strip naked and run through the streets of the town on the morning that the ice on the lake cracks, signaling the spring thaw. Chris leads the charge. One year, several cast members ran naked through the streets of Roslyn for the shooting of this scene. Roslyn's mayor and town council were not amused. (Courtesy of Roslyn Pubic Library.)

Barry Corbin (in front) portrays Maurice Minnifield, a patriotic ex-astronaut and millionaire entrepreneur. He owns the radio station, newspaper, and 15,000 acres of local land and sees Cicely as the new "Alaskan Riviera." John Cullum portrays Holling Vincoeur, a 62-year-old adventurer who gives up big-game hunting to settle down and run the local tavern. Holling has sworn off love until 18-year-old Shelly appears. (Courtesy of Roslyn Pubic Library.)

Peg Phillips portrays Ruth-Anne Miller, a sage 75-year-old who runs a one-stop shop that serves as grocery store, post office, library, and video store. Miller dispenses advice free with every purchase. She guides the townspeople through many unusual predicaments. When Phillips turned 65, she enrolled at the University of Washington's Drama School, hired an agent, and was an immediate sensation. (Courtesy of Roslyn Pubic Library.)

Darren Burrows, who plays Ed, the teenage Native American with an IQ of 180 and a yen for Hollywood, remembers, "I'm part Cherokee and Apache and my hair is on the blond side so every other episode I had to dye it black. I hated that part. It was weird to see myself with black hair." (Courtesy of Roslyn Pubic Library.)

In this episode, Cicely prepares for its annual Day of the Dead parade and Thanksgiving Day feast. The Native Americans celebrate the Mexican Day of the Dead by decorating the town, dressing up in costume, and having a parade. Joel receives news that because of the decline of the dollar, his service is worth less than when he signed his contract and he will have to remain in Cicely another year. (Courtesy of Roslyn Pubic Library.)

During the third season, Maggie's mother comes for a visit and announces that she and Maggie's father are divorcing after 32 years of marriage. Maggie is upset at the news and rushes out of her house, leaving her mother behind. However, while she is in town, her mother manages to set Maggie's house on fire, razing the structure and burning all of Maggie's possessions: her clothes, her furniture, and, worst of all, her dioramas of lost loves. (Courtesy of Roslyn Pubic Library.)

Darren Burrows plays the role of Ed Chigliak, a Native American who spends much of his time helping Dr. Joel get used to the ways of the residents in Cicely. Ed has an uncanny sense of timing and often appears out of nowhere with bits of wisdom—picked up from the many films he has watched. (Courtesy of Roslyn Pubic Library.)

Barry Corbin describes Maurice as "very American and patriotic. He's a retired astronaut who orbited the earth in a NASA capsule and Alaska is about the only place to contain his ego. There's another side to Maurice too. . . . as much as he's accomplished he's never lived up to his dad's expectations and he struggles with some insecurity but usually it's well masked by his huge ego." (Courtesy of Roslyn Pubic Library.)

Best Wishes Elaine Miles (signature)

Elaine Miles portrays Marilyn Whirlwind, Dr. Joel's stoic and quirky assistant. Marilyn's subtle calm is the perfect foil to Dr. Joel's neurotic behavior. Marilyn insists on becoming Dr. Joel's assistant and she rarely speaks, while Dr. Joel rarely stops talking. Born in Pendelton, Oregon, Miles was raised outside Seattle by a member of the Umatilla tribe. Miles had no previous acting experience when she was cast for the part of Marilyn. (Courtesy of Roslyn Pubic Library.)

John Corbett portrays Chris Stevens, Cicely's disc jockey. He quotes Walt Whitman, Shakespeare, and Tolstoy on air. Chris provides commentary on the goings on of Cicely's eccentric residents. He is also the town's only clergyman, ordained through an advertisement in *Rolling Stone* magazine. (Courtesy of Roslyn Pubic Library.)

It took eight days to shoot a *Northern Exposure* episode. Two or three of those eight days were spent filming in Roslyn, but home base was in the Seattle suburb of Redmond—where a 28,000-square-foot warehouse was converted into sets and a soundstage. Not all Roslyn residents and shopkeepers were excited about film crews moving in for days at a time for several years in a row. There were advantages—such as tourist dollars—and disadvantages—such as streets being closed off for several days in a row and businesses shut down—although businesses were paid well (more than they would normally have made in a day). Tour buses lined the streets, and Roslyn raked in millions in tourist dollars as a result of the show.

NORTHERN EXPOSURE

RESIDENTS, GUESTS AND VISITORS OF ROSLYN

We are pleased to announce that our cast and crew will be filming in Roslyn on the following dates. The times given are approximate.

**Tuesday September 8th 8:00am to 9:00pm
Wednesday September 9th 6:00am to 9:00pm
Thursday September 10th 6:00am to 9:00pm**

We would also like to apologize, in advance, for any inconvenience that our filming may cause. And, we would like to thank you for your understanding, continued support, and cooperation, which has helped make *Northern Exposure* the successful television series it has become, as evidenced by our recent Emmys.

Also, our sincere thanks for your cooperation with the street closure during the parade.

Pipeline Productions, Inc.
7140 180TH Avenue N.E., Redmond, WA 98052-4972
206/869-7535   Fax 206/869-1333

Rob Morrow's character, Dr. Joel Fleishman, is a young Jewish doctor from New York City who is bound by contract to practice medicine in the remote Alaskan town of Cicely for four years to repay his student loans. He struggles to work in a makeshift doctor's office surrounded by oddball locals. (Courtesy of Roslyn Pubic Library.)

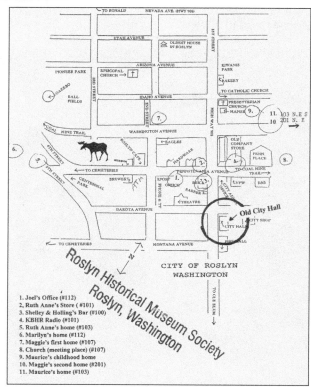

Much of the filming for *Northern Exposure* was done in Roslyn, and existing structures in the town were used. With this map, people can visit all their favorite characters' homes, hangouts, and businesses.

In May 1995, CBS tossed *Northern Exposure* to the wolves. The end was expected by the cast. "It was so sad," said Peg Phillips, who played Ruth-Anne Miller. "I had to leave in a hurry. I said, 'Goodbye, darlings, I've got to get out of here before I cry.' A series just takes up your whole life. You form attachments. And then it's gone. It was very, very difficult emotionally." (Courtesy of Roslyn Pubic Library.)

A generous thanks to those who make up Roslyn's remarkable history—from generations past to the present—for making Roslyn the amazing place it is. Roslyn has become a part of me, my adopted hometown.

—Jaymi Trimble

Pictured on this page is the Roslyn Gang, who helped make this book possible by supporting the author with their amazing talents and tireless effort. Here author Jaymi Trimble and her daughter Lyndseigh Trimble Mahan (see acknowledgments) stand in the Old Roslyn Jail, established in 1908. This is the same cell Willie Craven (Washington's first black mayor) accidentally got locked in as a kid. "That liked to scared me to death. We didn't mess around down there no more," recalls Craven. (Courtesy of Jay DeBoer.)

One of the joys C. Thomas finds in photography is the challenge of bringing his subjects to life . . . which is especially challenging considering one of his favorite places to shoot is the cemetery. C. Thomas is also an experienced iconographer. He contributed several images for the book. See acknowledgments and also visit his Web site at www.cthomascooney.com.

Visit us at
arcadiapublishing.com